Amok

Jessica Mayhew
Amok

20/20 **EYEWEAR**
PAMPHLET SERIES
2015

First published in 2015 by Eyewear Publishing Ltd
74 Leith Mansions, Grantully Road
London W9 1LJ United Kingdom

Typeset with graphic design by Edwin Smet
Printed in England by Lightning Source
All rights reserved © 2015 *Jessica Mayhew*

The right of Jessica Mayhew to be identified as author of this work has been asserted in accordance with section 77 of the Copyright, Designs and Patents Act 1988

ISBN 978-1-908998-76-7
WWW.EYEWEARPUBLISHING.COM

Thanks to
KA, KM and MM.

Dedicated to K.A, who found these places with me.

Table of contents

- 9 *Rainy Season*
- 10 *Amok*
- 11 *Loi Kratong*
- 12 *In The Mountains*
- 13 *Old Quarter*
- 14 *Mangroves*
- 15 *Medical Museum*
- 16 *Purlicue*
- 17 *Offerings*
- 18 *Chickens*
- 19 *Golden Virginia*
- 20 *Parents*
- 21 *Once, in an office*
- 22 *Hibernation*
- 23 *Death Of The Egyptian's Husband*
- 24 *Spirit Houses*
- 25 *Inside The Belly Of An Ox*
- 26 *One Hand Clapping Is Not*
- 27 *New Cities*
- 28 *Satnav*

Rainy Season

Monks stay put
so they don't harm the shoots.
We trawl through gutter-run
the colour of precious wood
for another meal of rice
while cockroaches tide up walls
above the flood line.
Fon tok, rain tongue
spitting on a foot of soi water,
lightning I cannot pronounce
but count, gaining ground
each time saffron dusk cracks –
five miles, four miles, three.
We lie with windows open,
swiping mosquitoes we can only hear
and smear someone else's blood,
mingled with mine, down white paint.
When I sleep, the rain
is bats back home
that have somehow learned to sing
the splashy notes of blackbirds
decked with frost, a proper October.
Here, alms bowls fill
with baht and water,
monks crouch, protected by the blue
of old tattoos, the five lines,
Buddha, serene, around every neck,
but all this season, your chest when bare, was wet.
We should make an amulet of the rain.

Amok

Here, the fish is steamed
in a woven basket of leaves.
Candles crimson through paper,
belled into lanterns
strung stagewards.

Light blanks the hung sheet,
while behind it, the children
are blind, or deaf.

Drums. Figures flee from home.
Two monkeys fight to the death.
One buffalo, held too far off
fades into static. Strings whine.

Six thousand miles away,
in the kind of place
that still has last year's tinsel
caught in tape above the doorframe,
you sit and twist your wedding ring
like a dial, trying to bring something else
back into focus.

Loi Kratong

Wrapped in silk, we walked to the moat.
Children surfaced like seals,
splashed after floats to sink them.

We lit candles on the water,
wicks almost too damp to catch.

I kept my wish on my tongue.

The next day, men with bamboo poles
and rolled-up sleeves
fished for remains,

petals, banana leaves, pins.
The river spirit, too, was quiet.

Whatever you wished for, say it again.

In The Mountains

The road so steep we almost didn't make it,
locals on mopeds going by, in low gears,
gawking. We couldn't find the waterfall,
but lay down, sweat-soaked on the flat,
black-veined rocks by the river. Eyelids lit
pink, skin hot all over. Our sometimes glances
snaring neon butterflies or birds.

Later, we drank the last of the beers warm,
watching clouds foam above the mountains,
then drain, sky to line, the river gargling stones.
Our under-eyes scoured red. But we watched
the stars roam up, as I remembered doing
as a child, naming them as if they were fixed.

Old Quarter

Past herbs, ground bones, shrivelled skins
in jars, we stepped into constant traffic,
motorbikes leaning around us
like a red sea in an old book.

Shops were shuttered by ten
as we walked back with the rats,
hotel already dark and locked,
casket-makers opposite:
black boxes, gold handled, stacked.

Laughing, I laced my fingers
to boost you over the wall,
my face against your stomach,
your lung's pull, things that
will only last as long as you do.

Mangroves

This crushed mosquito is just debris
held together by my blood

clotting in the mangroves
for maybe a thousand years or more,

the icecube melts in my mouth
inside a sip of whisky

while I float in dimming water,
amber-tongued

slurring stars through waves
and watching pale crabs

sidle to surf, warm
as sun-licked resin

before a ritual of mangroves
fingers buckled against ground

like ancients crouched
on their haunches

caught rising from sleep
eyes held against the thinning dark.

Medical Museum

Parasites, suicides,
skin flayed on tarmac

or else crushed, bones broken.
In another room: babies, pickled.

Little ones with open chests,
swollen heads, left with toys

and flowers at their feet.
Next door, three murderers

like sleeping commuters
at train windows,

collapsed against the glass
that encases them,

still oozing fat into a tray.
The notice states

they stood to die, blindfolded,
lotus cupped in their hands,

the sudden shot.
They grin, *live with this, then.*

Purlicue

Places it wasn't proper
to hold hands, even,
we stood apart to study maps
in shaded courtyards,
capillaries of borders, roads,
rivers traced in broad blue strokes.

Like any city, by evening
I would know again
the cartography of edges,
the smudge of your mouth
on the beer bottle's rim.
Alone, we devise our own scale,
down to the way your hand draws
the curtain, brings on the dark.

Offerings

They released turtles here
twice a year, they held up
the unpuzzled shells.

Under the village gate
demons leered, draped in silk
to scare worse things away.

We sipped *Bintang*
rapped our knuckles on the table
when we mentioned missing planes,

murders on midnight beaches.
Offerings were everywhere,
banana leaves frayed on sand,

on the red roads,
ashed incense below puce hills,
balls of rice on grey stone.

Our rooms too, you'd lose coins
stamped with beasts or kings,
or shed coppers on bus seats,

and in the morning I'd find
a coin printed in reverse on my thigh
silver through the bed sheets.

Chickens

Fish, bellies grinning, lie out on mats,
scales winking on the women's hands,
their foreheads too, when they raise
their wrists to dab at sweat. Noontime,
and I can taste the guts in the drain,
meat hanging from the roof to dry
above bright fruit, curled pig skin,
hairy hooves of coconut.
We are walking through blood,
bent under low ceilings, naked bulbs,
while the locals laugh. Two chickens,
tied, spasm against my legs,
then the keeper draws them up,
passes a small blade across their necks.

Golden Virginia

In the yellow field, you taught me to roll your cigarettes.

To lip the filter
and pincer tobacco,
slouching against your car bonnet,
hot but jazz-clicking to cool.

I brush the final dottle
from my sleeves to the thermals,
where one by one, crows out-race themselves,
hacking their names. They can be tamed,
you say, taught a tongue
and they will forget their own.

Down by the tyres, it is damp,
stems crushed and zig-zagged with tread.

The occasional nip of nettles
raises a Braille I will read tomorrow.
Sheep stud the hill like pulled teeth.

Thumb-nick to lighter wheel
strikes an after-image,
the childish trick of rubbing my eyes
to find faces in light.
                There. There.
And there's the sun,
peeking over cowslip, and corn gone to seed.
From the ground, not everything is gold
and the earth tilts again to bring us to our names.

Parents

It seemed like they were up all night,
a place we were only allowed to visit
on New Year's Eve, or parties
where we'd succumb, fall asleep under forts of coats.

A midnight room, lit by television only,
legs tangled, wine all drunk,
we'd pause, blinking in the doorway,
hands rolled in sleeves before we walked in.

It was something we owed them.
Our time, while we stood upstairs,
foreheads pressed to banisters, but still they'd hear us,
call, *Enough now, it's getting late.*

Once, in an office

still tanned from a year
of reading signs like a child,
letters unknown, curled snakes
on platters, raw sun striking
carvings that almost weren't there,
then thinking of home on the wade to the boat,
shorts soaked, bucked from the shore despite the storm,
while lightning lashed sand. The threat of glass –

she saw the solicitor bite the end
of the pen, make the divide,
and realised she wasn't homesick
for that place, or people
but a time.

Hibernation

Raking, she found a hedgehog
in deep winter sleep.
Next day, on the train to London

she couldn't shift the memory
of that thorned body, desires
that lulled it under frost.

In five o'clock dark,
jacketed, she avoided the parks,
the sleeping bag torn at the taxi rank,

but Tube-bound with cold hands,
found the yawning Underground.
Waiting for the Central line,

eyes closed, she felt the weight
above of the coming snow,
bone white, an almost-death.

Commuters covered her with leaves
of newspaper. By morning,
the city was pale all over.

Death Of The Egyptian's Husband

Cleopatra-kohled
on the night of her sixty-eighth birthday,
she said again how she would not pass through
Pembrooke Avenue, to see her ex-husband's house.
Instead, he would always be drinking
in her old kitchen,
watching the ice in his scotch
while onions grizzled on the hob
and the beech leaves moored on the lawn outside,
looked just like the boats at Alexandria.

Spirit Houses

The dead return to us in dreams,
shunning golden spirit houses
on every corner, and the offerings:
incense, too-green Fanta,
Buddha's half-lid gaze.

Just like you,
being five months dead,
returning in the stammered ammo
of a bird, shadowing the plastic roof,
claws a promise of rain.

Often speaking, as a girl in Shetland,
of the German pilot swooping low,
his ghost-cross bent across
grass and rock, the shagged coast,
and him being close enough
that seventy years later
you could still describe your running,
and his red hair.

Inside The Belly Of An Ox

No labour to slip inside,
one foot braced
on the row of teeth
like broken stones,
the massive tongue.
A lung's-worth to slide
down the gullet to the belly.
So dark, you must imagine
hooves sparking against flint,
sun on curved spine,
your tail losing against spiralling flies.

You might expect two eye-holes
to let in light, like a child's Halloween mask,
but you are far too deep for that.
Just the wet flex of muscle,
sweating against cart-rope
as if you haul the whole earth
underfoot, two thousand temples,
as old as the grass, the dust,
the bone of your horn, found lying
in ochre and carved by the hunter.
Even as Orion rises above parched trees,
you pause and remember,
the spilt blood, the rough blushed walls.

One hand clapping is not

  three pigeons
dancing in the branches

  a dark-barked apple tree
wet on the equinox

  dew whitening to frost
to cloud and back to ground

  stone shifting
to sand against the window

  people testing snow
with outstretched hands

New Cities

Begin with a barefoot child,
see him chase a kite through red dust,
the kind that muddies the skies.
                          Now go back to blue,
lizard-tongue hue, the curve
of a tail past the dead dog
in the river, bloated and peeled,
bald as the novices who giggled upstairs
above palaces, graves.

Faster, now, imagine rain coaxing teeth
from soil, a rib, so ease your way
to squat on pavement with a flat beer
below yellow houses that were once French.
                          Go further, double lanterns
in a swollen river. A dragon bridge.
Know how all cities shift to slake your taste,
buck their moorings like ships,
lean away from home.   Remember
a red bridge,   slow dog,   blue kite,
a child's bones.

Satnav

Bleeping. The satnav insisting there was a route through,
gone only a year, and the road dug up,
poppies already rooted. Tarmac ended at mud,
crows made chevrons above the field,
car sloughing through rain at the camber.

You were still miles away. Further, the satellite rambled,
remembering the old road like a star, long dead.
I could do with a map, those giant books my dad
would produce from under the seat,
bloated with damp, on those journeys that needed

a turn of the page. I pull over to call you.
I'm lost. Where are you? I don't know.
Your voice still amused. Far past your house,
I think of those satellites, machines on an unmade road,
and what's beyond that I do not think about.

Acknowledgments are due to the editors of
Ambit and *Stand Magazine* where versions of some
of these poems have previously appeared.

EYEWEAR PUBLISHING

EYEWEAR 20/20 PAMPHLET SERIES

BEN STAINTON EDIBLES
MEL PRYOR DRAWN ON WATER
MICHAEL BROWN UNDERSONG
MATT HOWARD THE ORGAN BOX
RACHAEL M NICHOLAS SOMEWHERE NEAR IN THE DARK
BETH TICHBORNE HUNGRY FOR AIR
GALE BURNS OPAL EYE
PIOTR FLORCZYK BAREFOOT
LEILANIE STEWART A MODEL ARCHAEOLOGIST
SHELLEY ROCHE-JACQUES RIPENING DARK
SAMANTHA JACKSON SMALL CRIES
V.A. SOLA SMITH ALMOST KID
GEORGE SZIRTES NOTES ON THE INNER CITY
JACK LITTLE ELSEWHERE
DAMILOLA ODELOLA LOST & FOUND
KEITH JARRETT I SPEAK HOME
JESSICA MAYHEW AMOK
JULIE MORRISSY I AM WHERE
MICHAEL NAGHTEN SHANKS YEAR OF THE INGÉNUE
ALICE WILLINGTON LONG AFTER LIGHTS OUT

SHORTLISTED FOR THE MICHAEL MARKS PUBLISHERS' AWARD 2015

Printed by Libri Plureos GmbH in Hamburg, Germany